TO

THE DEEVO MAN

Tom Wolfe is the author of *The Electric Kool-Aid Acid Test,*
The Pump House Gang, Radical Chic & Mau-Mauing the
Flak Catchers, The Kandy-Kolored Tangerine-Flake
Streamline Baby, The Right Stuff and numerous articles.

'YER BROTHER
JESUS TIME 1982

Also by Tom Wolfe
in Picador
The New Journalism

Tom Wolfe

IN OUR TIME

PICADOR
published by Pan Books

First British publication 1980 in Picador by Pan Books Ltd,
Cavaye Place, London SW10 9PG
Copyright © 1961, 1963, 1964, 1965, 1968, 1971, 1972, 1973, 1975, 1976,
1977, 1978, 1979, 1980 by Tom Wolfe
Designed by Sheila Wolfe
ISBN 0 330 26224 6
Printed in the United States of America by
The Maple-Vail Book Manufacturing Group, Binghamton, N.Y.

"Stiffened Giblets" first appeared, in a slightly different form, in *Life*.
"Entr'actes and Canapés" first appeared in *Esquire*, also in a slightly
different form. Acknowledgment is also made to *The American Spectator*,
the *Chicago Tribune*, *The Critic*, the *Daily Telegraph* (London), the *New
York Herald Tribune*, *Venture Magazine*, and *The Washington Post*, where
some of these drawings first appeared

Special thanks are due to *Harper's*, where the feature called "In
Our Time" originated, and where the drawings on pages 2, 6, 12, 24–54,
and 70 first appeared

Lupum auribus tenes
S.B.W.

CONTENTS

IN OUR TIME

"I got this supervisor where I work—these middle-age people, man, they're like children. All they think about is sex and dope. He's always coming around with this little grin on his face, talking about amyl nitrite and PBD. I mean, that's what you do in the fuckin' ninth or tenth grade, man."

1   Stiffened Giblets

For me the 1970s began the moment I saw Harris, on a little surprise visit to the campus, push open the door of his daughter Laura's dormitory room. Two pairs of eyes popped up in one of the beds, blazing like raccoons' at night by the garbage cans . . . illuminating the shanks, flanks, glistening haunches, and cloven declivities of a boy and girl joined mons-to-mons. Harris backed off, one little step after another. He looked as if he were staring down the throat of a snake. He pulled the door shut, ever so gingerly.

The girl in the bed was not his daughter, but that didn't calm him in the slightest. For an hour we lurched around the campus, looking for Laura. Finally we went back to her room, on the chance she might have returned. This time Harris knocked on the door, and a girl's voice said, "Come in." Quite a cheery voice it was, too.

"Laura?"

But it wasn't Laura. Inside, in the bed, was the same couple—except that they were no longer *in medias res*. They were sitting with the covers pulled up to about collarbone level, looking perfectly relaxed. *At home,* as it were.

"Hi," says the girl. "Can we help you?"

Their aplomb is more than Harris can deal with. He takes on the look of a man who, unaccountably, feels that *he* has committed the gaffe. He begins to croak. He sounds ashamed.

"I'm Laura's . . . I'm looking for my . . . I want . . ."

"Laura's at the library," says the boy. He's just as relaxed and cheery as the girl.

Harris backs out and closes the door once more . . . very diffidently . . . At the library we find his missing daughter. She has long, brown Pre-Raphaelite hair, parted in the middle, a big floppy crew-neck sweater, jeans, and clogs. She's eighteen years old and looks about twelve and is not the least bit embarrassed by what her father tells her.

"Daddy, really. Don't pay any attention to that," she says. "I mean, my *God,* everybody used to have to use the *kitch*en! There was a mattress on the floor in there, and you used to have to jump over the mattress to get to the refrigerator-sort-of-thing. So we made a schedule, and everybody's room is a Free Room a couple of days a month, and if your room's a Free Room, you just go to the library-sort-of-thing. I mean, the kitchen was . . . *so . . . gross!*"

All Harris does is nod slowly, as if some complex but irresistible logic is locking into place. In the time it takes us to drive back to New York, Harris works it out in his mind . . . The kitchen was *so gross*-sort-of-thing . . . That's all . . . By nightfall he has dropped the entire incident like a rock into a lake of amnesia.

By the next morning he has accepted the new order of things as *the given,* and in that moment he becomes a true creature of the 1970s.

How quickly we swallowed it all over the past ten years! I keep hearing the 1970s described as a lull, a rest period, following the uproars of the 1960s. I couldn't disagree more. With the single exception of the student New Left movement—which evaporated mysteriously in 1970—the uproars did not subside in the least. On the contrary, their level remained so constant, they became part of the background noise, like a new link of I–95 opening up.

The idea of a coed dorm, with downy little Ivy Leaguers copulating in Free Rooms like fox terriers, was a lurid novelty even as late as 1968. Yet in the early 1970s the coed dorm became *the standard.* Fathers, daughters, faculty—no one so much as blinked any longer. It was in the 1970s, not the 1960s, that the ancient wall around sexual promiscuity fell. And it fell like the walls of Jericho; it didn't require a shove. By the mid-1970s, anytime I reached a city of 100,000 to 200,000 souls, the movie fare available on a typical evening seemed to be: two theaters showing *Jaws,* one showing *Benji,* and eleven showing pornography of the old lodge-smoker sort, now dressed up in color and 35 mm. stock. Two of the eleven would be drive-in theaters, the better to beam the various stiffened giblets and moist folds and nodules out into the night air to become part of the American Scene. Even in the rural South the *typical* landscape of the 1970s included— shank to flank with the Baptist and United Brethren churches and the hot-wax car wash and the Arby's—the roadside whorehouse, a windowless shack painted black or maroon with a shopping mall–style back-lit plastic marquee saying: TOTALLY NUDE GIRL MASSAGE SAUNA & ENCOUNTER SESSIONS.

The wall around promiscuity was always intended to protect the institution of the family. In the 1970s one had a marvelous, even bizarre opportunity to see what happens to that institution when it is left unprotected. The 1970s will be remembered as the decade of the great Divorce Epidemic; or, to put it another way, the era of the New Cookie. The New Cookie was the girl in her twenties for whom the American male now *customarily* shucks his wife of two to four decades when the electrolysis gullies appeared above her upper lip. In 1976 Representative Wayne Hays of Ohio, one of the most powerful figures in the House of Representatives, was ruined when it was discovered that he had put his New Cookie, a girl named Elizabeth Ray, on his office payroll. It was this bureaucratic lapse that was his undoing, however, not the existence of the New Cookie. Six months before, when he had divorced his wife of thirty-eight years, it hadn't caused a ripple.

Ways of life that as late as 1969 had seemed intolerable scarcely drew a second glance in 1979. In 1969 I was invited to address a group of Texas corporation heads on the subject of "the drug culture." The meeting was held on the back lawn of the home of one of the group in a pavilion with a hardwood floor below and striped tenting above, the sort of rigging that is used for deb season dances in the fall. Why these eighty or ninety businessmen had erected this edifice to hear a talk about the dopers I couldn't make out . . . until one of them spoke up in the middle of my talk and said: "Listen, half the people here already know it, and so I'm gonna tell you, too: my son was arrested two nights ago for possession of marijuana, and that's the third goddamned time in ten goddamned months for that little peckerwood! Now . . . what are we gonna *do* about it!"

This was greeted with shouts of "Yeah!" . . . "Mine, too!" . . . "My daughter—four times, goddamn it!" . . . "You tell 'em, Bubba!" . . . "Form a mully-foggin' committee!"

Somehow I knew at that moment it was only a matter of time before the smoking of marijuana was legalized in the United States, and it had nothing to do with medical facts, juridical reasoning, or the Epicurean philosophies of the weed's proponents. It had to do solely with the fact that people of wealth

and influence were getting tired of having to extract their children from the legal machinery. That was getting worse than dope itself. By 1979 it had come to pass. My book *The Electric Kool-Aid Acid Test* had been about a man, the novelist Ken Kesey, who had been arrested twice in California for possession of a few ounces of marijuana. Facing a probable five-year jail sentence, he had fled to the jungles of Mexico to live among the dapple-wing anopheles, the *verruga*-crazed Phlebotomus, and Pacific Coast female ticks. That was in 1966. Today, on sunny days in Manhattan, one can see young office workers sitting on the Contempo Slate terraces out front of the glass buildings along Park Avenue and the Avenue of the Americas wearing Ralph Lauren Saville Pseud suits and Calvin Klein clings, taking coffee breaks and toking their heads off, passing happy sopping joints from fingertip to fingertip, and goofing in the open air. In New York, as in California and most other states, possession of a small amount of marijuana has been reduced to a misdemeanor and, in effect, taken off the books, since the police, with the tacit consent of the citizenry, usually ignore it.

As the moral ground shifted, like the tectonic plates of the earth, matters of simple decorum were not spared, either. To me the most fascinating side of

Watergate was the ease and obvious relish with which men and women on both sides of the Senate hearing room table and the bar of justice, the sheriffs as well as the bandits, the winners as well as the losers, capitalized on the event in the form of book deals and television commercials. The Watergate book was one of the decade's new glamour industries. For the losers—Haldeman, Ehrlichman, Magruder, McCord, Hunt, Nixon, John Dean, Mo Dean—it was a matter of paying the lawyers. The old motto of the big-time criminal lawyers was the same as the highwayman's, i.e., "Your money or your life," meaning, "Before I'll defend you, you have to sign over to me everything you own, including your house." In the 1970s that changed to "Your book contract or your life" (a matter that appears to be an underlying source of conflict between Patty Hearst and F. Lee Bailey). And the winners? His Honor Judge Sirica, His Probity Leon Jaworski, His Jurisprudence Samuel Dash . . . How piously they cranked out their best sellers! . . . It became perfectly okay, quite the acceptable thing, to *cash in on your life* as a guardian of integrity and the law. A job such as special Watergate prosecutor had a book-publishing value of $900,000 at the very least—provided prominent people were found guilty and their reputations were ruined. Presumably Jaworski never thought of that ahead of time, and it should be pointed out that he shunted his portion of the profits from his book into the Leon Jaworski Foundation, whatever that may be. But there was no law that said you had to suffer an attack of scruples, and precious few of the boys did.

Least of all, *the* great Capitol Hill hero of Watergate, Senator Sam Ervin of North Carolina. His choral comment during the Senate hearings—"I'm jes' a plain ol' country lawyer . . ."—became the very voice of probity. So in the 1970s, how should such an Elder of the Forum spend the honored years of his retirement? Why, sitting in front of the television camera, of course, collecting money for saying, "There are lots of places where folks don't know me at all . . . I recently got me an American Express card. With this, maybe they'll treat me like somebody important, though I'm jes' a plain ol' country lawyer from North Carolina. The American Express card. Don't leave home without it." *Ave atque vale,* Defender of the Constitution!

Selling off chunks of one's righteous stuff via television commercials became not merely acceptable but *conventional* behavior for famous people in the 1970s. In 1969 the first man to set foot on the moon, Neil Armstrong, delivered, via television, a cosmic symploce measuring the stride of mankind itself in the new age of exploration. In 1979 Armstrong was on television, in a Sales Rep sack suit delivering Cordobas, Newports, and Le Barons for the Chrysler Corporation. *Non sibi sed patriae,* Apollo!

The hedonism of the 1970s derives, in my opinion, from a development so stupendous, so long in the making, and so obvious that, like the Big Dipper or the curvature of the earth, it is barely noticed any longer. Namely, the boom of the booms. Wartime spending in the United States in the early 1940s brought the Depression to an end and touched off a boom that has continued for nearly forty years. The wave of prosperity had its dips, but they were mere wrinkles in a soaring curve. The boom pumped money into *every* class level of the population on a scale such as history has never known. Truck dispatchers, duplicator-machine repairmen, bobbin cleaners, policemen, firemen, and garbage men were making so much money—$15,000 to $20,000 (and more) per year—and taking so many vacations on tropical littorals and outfitting their $12,000 RVs with so many microwave ovens and sauna booths, it was impossible to use the word "proletarian" any longer with a straight face.

By the late 1970s these *new masses* began appearing also in France, West Germany, Switzerland, England, Norway, Sweden, Japan and, to a lesser extent, Italy—which is to say, throughout the *capitalist* world. By 1977 per capita incomes in these countries were catching up with those of the United States and outstripping the rate of inflation in most cases. In England the average family's "disposable" or "discretionary" income—the surplus wealth that new ways of living are made of—had risen 26.5 percent in ten years, and the increase was greatest among working-class people. It had become common for skilled workers to make as much as $20,000 a year, bringing them up even, in income, with middle-level executives and top corporate salesmen. In early 1979 the average hourly wage for workers in manufacturing plants was $6.49 in the United States, the same in West Germany, $7.29 in Norway, and $8.46 in Switzerland. Inflation was becoming a threat, but the European workers' second homes, sports cars, vacations in Venice, and calfskin trench coats were real.

The old utopian socialists of the nineteenth century—the Saint-Simons, the Owens, the Fouriers—*lived* for the day when industrial workers would command the likes of $6.49 or more per hour. They foresaw a day when industrialization (Saint-Simon coined the word) would give the common man the things he needed in order to realize his potential as an intelligent being: surplus (discretionary) income, political freedom, free time (leisure), and freedom from grinding drudgery. They never dreamed that their blissful utopia would be achieved not under socialism but as the result of a hard-charging, go-getter business boom. To heighten the irony, it was in the 1970s that socialism was dealt a blow from which it is never likely to recover. Starting with the publication of Solzhenitsyn's *Gulag Archipelago* in 1973, the repressive nature of socialism as a monolithic system of government became too obvious to ignore any longer. By the 1970s there was no possible ideological detour around concentration camps, and under genuine socialism the concentration camps were found again and again—in the Soviet Union, in Cambodia, in Cuba, in the new united Vietnam. By 1979 Marxism was finished as a spiritual force, although the ideologues lingered on. In objective terms, then, the time was ripe for a development that would have confounded all the twilight theories of the past one hundred years: namely, the Rise of the West. In subjective terms, however, the story was different. There was no moral force, no iron in the soul, not even a reigning philosophy, to give spiritual strength to the good times being had by all.

Solzhenitsyn, for his part, was not enchanted with American life, once he settled into his rural redoubt in Vermont. In his famous Harvard commencement speech of June 1978, he characterized the American way as soft, materialistic, morally impoverished. "The human soul," he said, "longs for things higher, warmer, and purer than those offered by today's mass living habits, introduced by the revolting invasion of publicity, by TV stupor, and by intolerable music. . . . Two hundred or even fifty years ago, it would have seemed quite impossible, in America, that an individual could be granted boundless freedom simply for the satisfaction of his instincts or whims." What Solzhenitsyn was looking at, utterly stupefied, was the first era of: *every man an aristocrat*.

In 1976 I wrote an essay entitled "The Me Decade and the Third Great Awakening." I soon found the phrase "the Me Decade" being used everywhere as a way of characterizing this as an age of narcissism, greed, or simple rut-boar wallowing. In the essay I was referring to something that I still find considerably more subtle:

America's extraordinary boom began in the early 1940s, but it was not until the 1960s that the *new masses* began to regard it as a permanent condition. Only then did they spin out the credit line and start splurging and experimenting with ways of life heretofore confined to the upper orders. In the 1970s they moved from the plateau of the merely materialistic to a truly aristocratic luxury: the habit of putting oneself on stage, analyzing one's conduct, one's *relationships,* one's hang-ups, one's personality, precisely the way noblemen did it during the age of chivalry. This secret vice was one of the dividends of the feminist movement of the 1970s. An ordinary status—woman, housewife—was elevated to the level of drama. One's existence as *a woman . . . as Me . . .* became something all the world analyzed, agonized over, drew cosmic conclusions from, or, in any event, took seriously. Books were written about *being a woman,* meetings were held, consciousnesses were raised (as the phrase went), television specials were produced, and magazines were founded upon that single notion. Every woman became a heroine of the great epic of the sexes. Out of such intense concentration upon the self, however, came a feeling that was decidedly religious, binding one beaming righteous soul to the other in the name of the cause.

And there you had the paradox of the 1970s: it was both the most narcissistic of decades and the least. In fact, such has been the paradox of hedonism itself for some 2,300 years. In the third century B.C. Epicurus, now remembered as the greatest of the hedonistic philosophers, lived a life that today would earn him the designation of "cult leader." At his home in Athens he established what would now be called a commune. The commingling of men and women within the Garden of Epicurus, as it was known, was viewed as depraved. Epicurus and his disciples developed the proposition that all truth is derived from the senses and the highest truth is derived from pleasure. Or as Hemingway would put it in our time: "Morality is what you feel good after." Yet the pursuit of pleasure, like most monomanias, carries the seeds of spirituality. Epicureanism became one of the most powerful pre-Christian religions, and in no time the Epicurean emphasis on pleasure became spiritual and, in fact, quite juiceless. Likewise, in the 1970s spirituality gushed forth in the most unexpected places, even among *swingers,* as the decade's most dedicated sexual-obsessives became known.

At a sex farm in the Santa Monica mountains of Los Angeles, people of all class levels gathered for weekends in the nude. They copulated in the living room, by the chess table, out by the pool, on the tennis courts, in the driveway, with the same open, free, liberated spirit as dogs in the park or baboons in a tree. In conversation, however, the atmosphere was quite different. The air became humid with solemnity. If you closed your eyes, you thought you were at a nineteenth-century Wesleyan church encampment at Oak Bluffs. It's the soul that gets a workout here, brethren . . . At the apex of my soul is a spark of the Divine . . . and I perceive it in the pure moment of ecstasy . . . which your textbooks call "the orgasm," but which I know to be Heaven . . .

And in this strange progress from sexology to theology was added another rogue surge to what I think of as the Third Great Awakening, namely, the third great religious wave in American history and the most extraordinary development of the 1970s. Such was the hunger for some form of spiritual strength that any obsession was sufficient to found a faith upon: jogging, flying, UFOs, ESP, health foods, or drug rehabilitation. No terrain was too barren or too alien to support a messiah. It was the Third Awakening that made possible the election as President of that curious figure Jimmy Carter, an evangelical Baptist

who had recently been "born again" and "saved," who had "accepted Jesus Christ as my personal Saviour." Jimmy Carter seemed to come straight from the tent meeting where Sister Martha played the Yamaha piano, and the sisters and the brethren stood up and gave witness and shouted, "Share it, brother! Share it, sister!" And praised God. In the four years that followed, Jimmy Carter wore the picnic clothes of the Atlanta suburbs and never seemed to understand the power that flowed through his pineywood veins. He dissipated the power and the glory and threw away all his trump cards. The people yearned for hallelujah, testifying, and the blood of the lamb, and he gave them position statements from the Teleprompter.

America now tingles with the things of the flesh while roaring drunk on things of the spirit. We are in that curious interlude of the twentieth century that Nietzsche foretold in the 1880s: the time of the *reevaluation,* the devising of new values to replace the osteoporotic skeletons of the old. God is dead, and forty new gods live, prancing like mummers. Behold, it is not the ending but the beginning! Ecce America—in her Elizabethan period, her Bourbon Louis romp, her season of rude animal health and rising sap! Sisters and brethren, it is written that these are evil days, but I say unto you: The holiest of spirits are even now bubbling up into every brain . . .

A Problem in Etiquette

In which the guest of honor, the famous architect, asked if he could
"bring someone," and the host and hostess try to decide if they dare seat
Someone between Chuck Brassbender of Morgan Guaranty and
Harmsden Grousestalker of Sullivan & Cromwell, as originally planned.

2   Entr'actes and Canapes

DISCO

The press was never very candid about Studio 54, which was Disco Fever's chronically inflamed viral center. We were told only that Studio 54 was the hot ticket at night for every sort of celebrity in New York, from Vitas Gerulaitis and Dolly Parton to Laurance Rockefeller, and a Land of Cockaigne for the high and the groovy. But you only had to spend an evening there yourself to see that it was much stranger than that: of the thousand-or-so souls on the dance floor at any one time, 750 were men, young and old, wearing strap undershirts, string vests, leather wristlets, and other Under the Expressway gear and bobbing up and down to seamless music and exploding lights in a dance called the pogo and pouring libido as lubricious as peanut oil over one another. Ever since the Second World War, the reigning styles in popular music, dress, and dance have tended to be created by marginal or outcast groups. Negroes (the term then) and poor whites (some of them from Liverpool) created rock. New Jersey teenage juvies brought about the drastic change in dance styles that began with the twist at the old Peppermint Lounge. And the male-homosexual netherworld created disco. The discotheque is the 1970s' quotidian and commercial ritualization of what used to be known as a homosexual rout, a fact that generally has not been laid on Mom & Dad & Buddy & Sis as they drive the Bonneville over to the mall to take disco lessons so they'll be ready for the Vesper Disco nights at the church in Lubbock, De Kalb, Grand Forks, Riverhead, or wherever.

PUNK

The greatest and most luridly putrid protagonist of Punk in America was John Simon Ritchie, an Englishman who renamed himself Sid Vicious. Punk had no American roots at all. It was a concept that had vitality only as a gob of spit, a sopping lunger, in the face of the British class system. American children had to read about it in *People* or *Vogue* in order to know what to wear or how to act. The 1960s became known as an era of "pseudo-events," events that took place only so the press could cover them. The 1970s did that one better and became the era of Knockoff Pseud, forms of life that existed *nowhere* but *in print* but were then acted out by people who believed they were real. Sid Vicious's great misfortune was in believing that Punk in America was real just because he was its star. He really believed that the Sic Fucks, who played at CBGB and OMFUG, and the Dead Kennedys, who played at Hurrah, meant every minute of it. He really *did* have a girlfriend named Nancy Spungen. He really did slice his wrists and overdose on heroin and die young to make a good-looking corpse. Incredible.

UPSTAIRS, DOWNSTAIRS

During the 1970s it dawned on me that PBS stood not for Public Broadcasting Service but for Petroleum's British Subsidiary. Every drama I watched was from England; every accent was British; and after every show a little sign appeared on the screen: "This program was made possible by a grant from the Exxon Corporation," if it wasn't Mobil.

GEORGE McGOVERN

In 1972 the most exquisite form of torture imaginable would have been to have found yourself locked inside a Seaboard railroad roomette just north of Jacksonville on the Miami-to-New York run with the radiator sizzling in an amok, red-mad psychotic overboil and George McGovern sitting beside you, telling you his philosophy of government. McGovern was very much like Henry Wallace, a man of aerial, even ethereal, intentions who was so boring he made your skull feel as if it were imploding. McGovern said everything in an earnest whine. Some orators' words catch fire; McGovern's were fireproof. They seemed to be made of Structo-Lite.

GATSBY

I'll never forgive the 1974 movie version of *The Great Gatsby,* which was the Fitzgerald novel as reinterpreted by the garment industry. Throughout the picture Robert Redford wore white suits. They fitted so badly that every time he turned a corner there was an eighty-microsecond lag before they joined him. Nevertheless, *Gatsby,* followed as it was nearly four years later by *Saturday Night Fever,* ruined one of the main joys of my life: wearing white suits. Pretty soon you saw white suits everywhere. They came crawling out of every shopping mall disco boutique in America on the backs of the Gold Chains in the Chest Hair set.

ELVIS

A producer for Columbia Records once explained the Elvis phenomenon to me as follows: "We had always known that R & B [rhythm and blues] had great potential, but it was what was known as race music. All the performers were Negroes, and all the audience were Negroes. We were waiting for a white Negro, so to speak, a white performer who knew how to use that sound. Presley was the man." But just how much *more* Presley represented didn't become clear until his death in 1977, which touched off an emotional blowout that rivaled those that followed the deaths of Franklin Roosevelt and Martin Luther King, Jr. Presley was the man who had at last pulled the black tie and Fred Astaire dancing pumps off popular music for whites. The fox trot's pretensions to fanlight-ballroom elegance disappeared under the Thom McAn bluchers. Presley had become a Valentino for poor whites. A genuine Tupelo boy raised on drop biscuits, loose sausage, Nabs & Coke, had entered Show Business heaven. The lubberly Shellube Pit down-home bubbas Presley insisted on keeping in his entourage were the despair of impresarios and hotel managers, but Presley's po' white legions loved him for it right up to the edematous end.

JONESTOWN

Among other things Jonestown was an example of a definition well known to sociologists of religion: a cult is a religion with no political power. Usually this is observed when the religion is in its ascendancy and is elevated from the status of "cult" to that of "church" or "denomination." The history of the Mormons in the nineteenth century is the prime example. The Reverend Jim Jones and his People's Temple, on the other hand, are examples of how to reverse the process in a single decade. As long as Jones & Company were going strong in San

Francisco and were an electoral mainstay of politicians at the state and the city levels, the People's Temple was a church and nothing else but. After Jonestown, the outfit was turned into a cult—"cult" was in every headline—like a werewolf that missed the predawn punch-in. Jones himself instantly became a "madman"—another word in every headline. In the 1970s, anyone who did anything evil enough became a madman. There were members of the press who spent months following Nixon's resignation trying to compile evidence of his insanity—in the face of every indication that he took the heat with rather remarkable aplomb. It is very comforting to believe that leaders who do terrible things are, in fact, mad. That way, all we have to do is make sure we don't put psychotics in high places and we've got the problem solved.

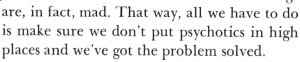

DESIGNER JEANS

Since the French Revolution clothing styles have provided a classic example of the trickle-down concept. The rich had clothes made by couturiers, tailors, or designers, and the masses wore knockoffs of same. That held true until the 1960s, when certain staples of High Bohemia began to be hauled up the scale from the land of the proles. Tops on the list in the 1970s—and the greatest testament to how credulity and wealth (i.e., fools and money) walk tall in our time—were designer jeans. I once indulged in a little (I thought) hyperbole about "prewashed prefaded two-tone tie-dyed patched-and-welted velvet-hand elephant-bell hip-hugging blue jeans with a procession of aluminum studs down the outseams and around the pockets in back bought for $49.95 at the New Groovissimo boutique." Well, that merely illustrates Philip Roth's (and Malcolm Muggeridge's) crack about the paucity of the writer's imagination in the face of the true stories of the twentieth century. No sooner do you think you have hit upon a piece of Rabelaisian hyperbole for our times than reality shrinks you like a wool sock. Studded designer jeans at $49.95 would be cheap.

MONDO BRANDO

During the 1970s the number of American movies shrank sharply, and the commercial pressure to make each one a blockbuster, as the phrase went, became intense. The only way to make sure the huge initial investment in a movie was not lost was to see to it that the picture secured play dates (bookings) in thousands of theaters around the world, in Manila and Valparaiso as well as Milwaukee and Victorville. The best way to secure the thousands of play dates was to have an internationally popular star in the cast. Only a handful of performers, most of them male, filled the bill: Redford, Newman, McQueen, Brando, Eastwood, Bronson. What such a King of the Play Dates did in a movie was not so important as his being there at all. Hence the role of Brando in the movie *Apocalypse Now*. He turns up in the last act as a mumblebum with his head shaved and his chin hooked down over his clavicle, whispering into his sternum. Play Date Kings can afford any eccentricities they please. Brando received $3 million for three weeks' work. Lately, however, there has been panic in the golden kingdom. The Redfords, Newmans, and McQueens have made so much money, they have been able to rest for years—four, five, six years—between movies. Meantime the movie audience has become ever younger and now falls mainly between the ages of fifteen and twenty-eight. Many of those children standing out there in the line in their down-filled jackets and polished chintz New Wave pants have never seen a Robert Redford or Steve McQueen movie. REDFORD . . . McQUEEN . . . It might as well be VALENTINO . . . or BARRYMORE . . . or some other name from out of the lint of a senile past.

THE DIGITAL CALCULATOR

This marvelous machine was the 1970s' most notable contribution to the impressive list of time-and-labor-saving devices that have made it possible for Americans, since the Second World War, to waste time in job lots and get less and less done—with sleekness and precision of style. The time you can waste (I speak from experience) going chuk, chuk, chuk, chuk on your calculator and watching the little numbers go dancing across the black window—all the while feeling that you are living life at top speed—is breathtaking. Earlier additions to the list: the direct-dial long-distance telephone, the Xerox machine, the in-office computer, the jet airliner (not to mention the Concorde). The jet airliner, for example, encourages you to drop everything, hop on a plane, and go to Los Angeles, or wherever, at a moment's notice. Later on you can't understand how the better part of a week got shot. In light of my own not exactly staggering literary output, I have become interested in the life of Balzac. I am convinced that the reason this genius was so productive—he published at least *sixty* books between ages thirty and fifty-one—was that he enjoyed no time- or labor-saving aids whatsoever, not even a typewriter. He dropped nothing and went nowhere on a moment's notice, not even to Maisons-Laffitte, which was twelve miles from Paris. He didn't ring up anybody in Brittany, much less London. He either wrote a note by hand or said the hell with it. *There* is a time-&-labor-saving device.

ROOTS

Alex Haley's purported history of his family from African village and slave boat to New York City and book contract brought the history of the novel full circle. In 1976 and 1977, *Roots* was a best seller—on the non-fiction list—for six months. In 1977, it won a special Pulitzer award for history. In the form of a seven-part television series in 1977, it drew an audience estimated by the A. C. Nielsen Company at 130 million, the biggest in the history of the medium. By the end of 1977, the roots of the book itself had begun to show. Haley had apparently helped himself to material from a novel called *The African,* by Harold Courlander. A British journalist went to Africa to retrace the steps of the clan Kinte-Haley and found out that much of what Haley wrote was based on made-up tales, to phrase it generously. All of which was in the grand tradition of the man most historians credit with having originated the modern novel, Daniel Defoe. In 1719, Englishmen were convinced that Defoe really had come across the diary of a shipwrecked sailor named Robinson Crusoe, just as, a few years later, they believed that Richardson's *Pamela* really was made up of anguished bulletins from a pretty girl living in the house of an aroused and hard-stalking middle-aged lecher.

PERRIER

In the fifties there was the martini. In the sixties there was vodka on ice. In the early seventies there was the glass of white wine. In the late seventies there was the bottle of Perrier, a French soda water. The fashionable American expense-account lunch drink became lighter and lighter, but not cheaper and cheaper. The soda water sold for $2.50 a glass in Manhattan restaurants.

LIGHT BEER

Even beer became lighter. The most successful new beers were diet beers, with all the body of Diet Shasta. To cloud men's minds lest they think there might be something effeminate about diet beer, the advertisers presented it on television in commercials that always showed the thin brew in the mitts of some famous jock who walked with a rolling sprung-thigh gait, as if he had two kegs of Dortmunder Dark suspended from his inguinal canal.

MUHAMMAD ALI

During the seventies professional boxing all but disappeared as an American sport outside of the heavyweight division. The last time I went to the fights at Madison Square Garden, which was in 1974, the crowd rose for a minute of silent prayer in memory of Juan Perón, who had died a week before. The last regular television broadcasts of boxing in the New York area—from Sunnyside Garden—were in Spanish. Latin and Italian fighters dominate the top ranks of virtually every division except the heavyweight, where black Americans rule. Or, rather, where one black American rules. True to his boast, Ali became the entire boxing franchise of the United States in the 1970s. The heavyweight division itself became the story of Muhammad Ali and his challengers, period. The publisher of one of the few remaining fight magazines told me: "The day Ali actually retires, I'm folding the magazine. If you can't put Ali on the cover, you can't sell a boxing magazine in America." But things may not be so grim after all. There may never be any way of knowing if Ali *has* actually retired.

SHORT HAIRCUTS

During the famous Hardhat Riot in New York in May of 1970, I was surprised to see miles and miles of long hair pouring out from under the hard hats of the construction workers and other proles who were busy creasing the skulls of antiwar students with helmets, pliers, clubs, and crowbars. My record for predictions has not been astounding, but on that very day I predicted that male college students would start wearing their

19

hair shorter, and the past ten years have borne me out. College boys have affected great Army Surplus Street People funkiness all that time, of course, but they do not *really* want to be mistaken for proles. So it's the shit kickers with their Camaros up on cinder blocks beefing up the suspension on Saturday afternoon in the Teen Burger hamlets of Oklahoma who now wear the hair of the much hated hippies of the 1960s, down to the shoulder blades, complete with headbands, while the college boys go in for the short, fluffy, thatchy look of Oxford undergraduates from the Evelyn Waugh period. Meantime, the shortest hair of all, the crew cut or butch cut—formerly associated with military macho—is now affected by the more trendy male homosexuals of the gay life.

THE FALL OF SOUTH VIETNAM

Both Le Duc Tho and Henry Kissinger declined to go to Stockholm to receive in person their Nobel prizes for the peace agreement of 1973 that "ended" the war in Vietnam. Obviously, neither had any taste for the ludicrous. Eighteen months later, the Soviet-supplied tanks rolled south, and scenes such as the Last Helicopter from Saigon were a good deal more grisly than the Last Train from Barcelona. The dominoes—as in "the much discredited domino theory"—fell, and the concentration camps went up, and Hanoi set about exterminating the Chinese of Vietnam, a parasitical race of congenital merchants and bourgeois bloodsuckers who refused to be assimilated into the new order, according to Hanoi. By then, the United States was no longer "intervening in the internal affairs of the Vietnamese people" nor fighting an "immoral war."

WOODY ALLEN

Woody Allen is the archetypal Hollywood figure of the 1970s, the New Yorker who wears an amused Upper Bohemian aloofness from Hollywood and goes to the Polo Lounge in night watchman pants and Keds basketball shoes. In movie circles today, any man who wears a suit, shirt, and tie is presumed to be on the premises as a representative of Wells Fargo or some other burglar alarm company. As the archetype, Allen wears the funkiest raiment of all in an era of Funky Chic: the sort of cheap plaid cotton shirt that was seen on math and chem majors at CCNY in the 1950s. He was on view regularly at the reigning Hollywood restaurant of the 1970s, Elaine's, which is not in Los Angeles but in New York—of course. In the old days of Café Society, the greatest treat in the world was to look across the velvet rope at El Morocco and see Bruce Cabot sitting at table number one with a tuxedo on and his teeth boiling and his irises lit up like flashlight bulbs and his hair plastered back like the Patent Leather Kid's. Today it's Woody Allen sitting in Elaine's at *his* table with his math-major outfit on and his head down, looking neither left nor right, as if *being noticed* were the last fate in the world he would want to encourage.

BRAIN PHYSIOLOGY

Freudianism was finally buried by the academic establishment in the 1970s, ending its forty-year reign in the United States. By 1979 Freudian psychology was treated only as an interesting historical note. The fashionable new frontier was the clinical study of the central nervous system, an attempt to map precisely how the panel is wired for fear, lust, hunger, boredom, or any other neural or mental event. Long overshadowed by psychoanalysis, brain physiology came into its own with the development of such equipment as the stereotactic needle implant. Today the new savants probe and probe and slice and slice and project their slides and regard Freud's mental constructs, his "libidos," "Oedipal complexes," and the rest, as quaint quackeries of yore, along the lines of Mesmer's "animal magnetism" and "*baquet* processes." The central concept of Freud's pathology, the "neurosis," is now regarded as a laughable historicism on the order of "melancholia" or "phlegmatism." Freud himself is regarded as an unusually humorless quack.

PEOPLE

The most successful new mass-circulation magazine, in a decade that was not always kind to mass-circulation magazines, was *People,* Time Inc.'s Pantagruelian offspring of *Time* magazine's one- or two-page back-of-the-book section called People. The success of *People* was due to three things: (1) It always showed you other people's living rooms (e.g., Mo Dean's as John headed off to jail); (2) it always showed you where other people's libidos were plugged in (e.g., there might be an article about a brain surgeon, but if he were polymorphous-perversely involved with a horse or a squash, *People* always ran a photograph of it); (3) it was a print annex to the TV set. Instead of ignoring television, *People* assumed that television was its audience's main interest, and people and *People* had to fit into the picture where they could. Rare was the issue that did not feature the likes of Phil Donahue, Miss Piggy, Carol Burnett, Robin Williams, or the Waltons on the cover. The idea was "You loved them on TV—now linger a moment over them in print."

THE FALL OF NIXON

The chief lesson of Watergate: the stability of the American political system is profound. It has a center of gravity like a 102-inch High Point Vinyleather sofa. The President of the Republic was forced from office, and as a result . . . *noth-*

ing happened . . . The tanks didn't roll, the junta delivered no communiqués from the Pentagon, the mobs didn't take to the streets, either before or after . . . Not even a drunk Republican ventured out to heave a brick through a head-shop window . . . Instead, everyone sat back and watched the show on television and enjoyed it tremendously. Then everybody sat back and watched Nixon's handpicked successor, Gerald Ford, do a pratfall from one side of the continent to the other and enjoyed that, too, as if he were William Bendix playing Chester Riley in *The Life of Riley*. Then, just to show how concerned they were about the steadiness of the ship of state, the citizens elected, off the wall, an unknown down-home matronly-voiced Sunday-schoolish soft-shelled watery-eyed sponge-backed Millennial lulu as the next President.

SIDEWALK STEREO

In the 1950s you could always tell cultivated people from proles, because cultivated people didn't watch television. In the 1960s, however, they caved in and even stopped lying to the survey takers about it. In the 1970s a new audiovisual cue was developed: the proles now went about the streets with 150-watt 100-decibel over-the-shoulder stereo radios and tape decks the size of storm-window salesmen's suitcases. By 1980 it had reached the point where if you caught anyone listening to popular music on the radio, any size radio, on the street, in the car, in the home, you knew you were in the presence of a stone prole skull.

THE YEAR THE NEW LEFT LEFT

One of the remarkable developments of the year 1970 was the disappearance of the New Left. Bango!—it was gone!—just like that. In May of 1970, the Movement, as it was known, had reached a peak of power and influence during the wave of campus disruptions that followed the shootings at Kent State and the invasion of Cambodia. By the fall, the Movement had evaporated. I have never understood how it happened. Many line troops in the Movement felt betrayed. In 1971, a student at the University of Rochester complained to me: "Last year, Jerry Rubin came here and told us we had to pull this rotten system up by the roots, there was nothing worth saving. This year, he came here and told us to *register to vote in the primary*." He gave the words about the same curdle one might have expected from Trotsky, Baader, or Meinhof. Eventually, Jerry Rubin trimmed his mane, cut off his beard, and enrolled in est. In 1970 Allen Ginsberg, hairiest of them all, made a dramatic appearance, with his beard totally shorn, and Abbie Hoffman had his long hair cut off on network television. So the haircut turned out to be, as the Dadaists used to say, a significant gesture. By 1979 there was no active left wing in America at all.

3   In Our Time

Those Whom God Hath Joined Together

"You've been living together for four years. Why get married now?"
"I'm tired of being snubbed by the doormen."

Mens Sana in Corpore Sano

"We'll give you a full scholarship, and you won't have to take but one class a week during basketball season, and you'll have your own apartment, rent-free, and eighteen hundred dollars a month for books, and a Corvette for yourself and a Caprice Classic for your folks, and when you graduate you'll be able to read the newspaper and the stereo ads and add and subtract on a portable calculator and direct-dial anywhere in the world."

The Birds and the Bees

"No, no, son, that's not how it works.
When you're forty-five or fifty, you'll get a new wife,
a young one, a girl in her twenties."

"What happens to the old one?"

"Well, she opens up a needlepoint shop and
sells yarn to her friends and joins a discussion group."

Nine Danger Signs for Wives

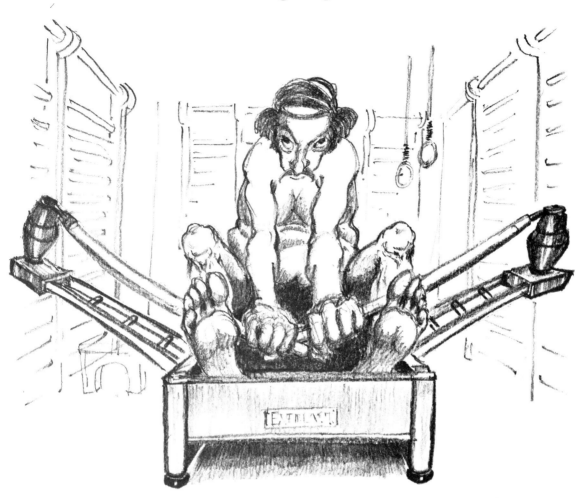

If your husband: (1) is between thirty-eight and fifty-four years old; (2) launches into an intense program of exercise; (3) starts losing weight and getting thin, whether through exercise or any other method; (4) begins using ever more ingenious and desperate means of covering his bald swath and goes to a hairstylist to have the results teased and fluffed for $17.50; (5) lets his mustache curl down at the ends (the so-called Zapata Look); (6) gives up his eyeglasses for soft contact lenses; (7) develops some completely new reading interest, such as art history, astrology, assertive therapy, Eastern philosophy, ecology, or the novels of Tom Robbins *(Even Cowgirls Get the Blues);* (8) starts leafing through your copies of *Vogue,* lingering over the ads; (9) begins having dreadful luck trying to catch the last flight back home from his business trips (airport fogged in, taxi had a flat tire, last-minute after-dinner meeting called, got all the way to the airport only to discover that the leather holder with all the credit cards was in the pocket of the bathrobe which was overlooked and left on the back of the bathroom door in the hotel room, and so on)—

then: (any of the above) he is fantasizing about a New Cookie; (any two of the above) he is looking for a New Cookie; (any three of the above or number seven or number nine by itself) he has found her; (any four of the above) she has sunk the hooks in; (any five or more of the above) he will have already started wrapping his eyebrows around his nose and trying to involve you in conversation about "our relationship."

The New Cookie

What are Mom & the
   Bonneville & Buddy & Sis
Up against a love like this?
That first night on
   the disco floor
She wore a pair
   of boxing trunks
While leather punks
   and painted lulus,
African queens
   and sado-zulus
Paid her court.
I grow old the 1970s way:
Deaf, but from a
   Max Q octaphonic beat,
Stroked out, but on
   my own two feet,
Disco macho!—for you,
   my New Cookie.

The Maternal Instinct

"How's your little boy?"

"Oh, I don't know what to do with him. He's sick, but he won't stay in bed. He had an angina attack sprinting on the beach, trying to impress the boys at his big conference. He had another one in his room trying to impress the little researcher I'm not supposed to know about. He had another one hanging some shutters in the kitchen trying to deal with his guilt."

Pedagogy

"Go ahead. Try me. The next one of you peckerwoods who sprays burning lighter fluid into my locker, boosts the tape deck out of my car or pees on the upholstery, hits me in the back of the head in the hallway with a johnny-mop canister or a urinal puck, tries any mackin' or jackin' in the back of the class, seals up this room with Krazy Glue so I can't get out, makes goomba-goomba sounds and asks the substitute teacher if she's got life insurance, or refers to me as "you mollyfoggin' lamehead," is gonna get a new hole in his nose."

The Joggers' Prayer

Almighty God, as we sail with pure aerobic grace and striped orthotic feet past the blind portals of our fellow citizens, past their chuck-roast lives and their necrotic cardiovascular systems and rusting hips and slipped discs and desiccated lungs, past their implacable inertia and inability to persevere and rise above the fully pensioned world they live in and to push themselves to the limits of their capacity and achieve the White Moment of slipping through the Wall, borne aloft on one's Third Wind, past their Cruisomatic cars and upholstered lawn mowers and their gummy-sweet children already at work like little fat factories producing arterial plaque, the more quickly to join their parents in their joyless bucket-seat landau ride toward the grave—help us, dear Lord, we beseech Thee, as we sail past this cold-lard desolation, to be big about it.

Great Moments in Contemporary Architecture

The Clients' First Night in the House

"Well, maybe we'll make *Architectural Digest* anyway."
"We damn well better."

Off to a Better Place

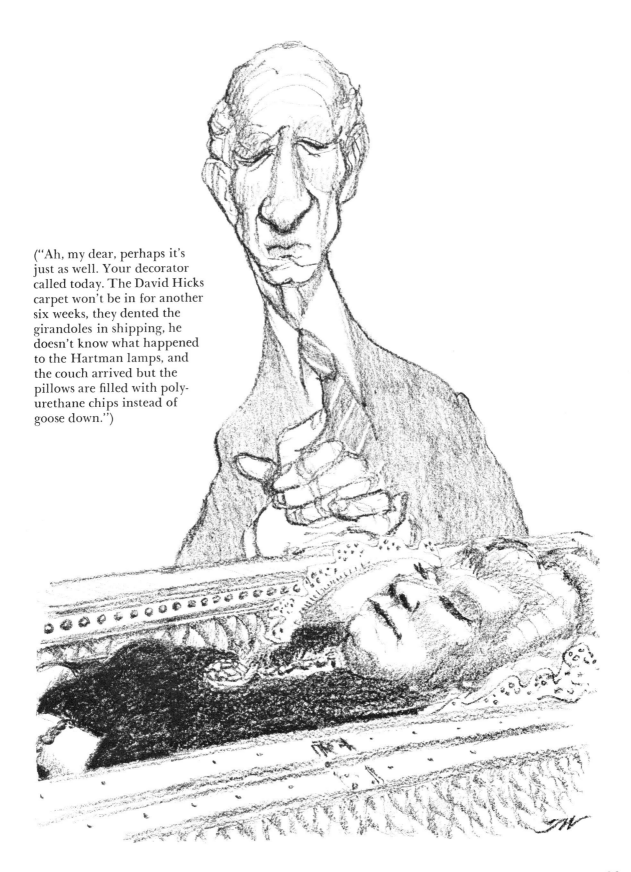

("Ah, my dear, perhaps it's just as well. Your decorator called today. The David Hicks carpet won't be in for another six weeks, they dented the girandoles in shipping, he doesn't know what happened to the Hartman lamps, and the couch arrived but the pillows are filled with polyurethane chips instead of goose down.")

The Invisible Wife

The Invisible Wife arrived at the party with Her Husband, but Her Husband was soon vectored off into another room by one of his great manswarm of chums, who began pouring an apparently delicious story down his ear.

The Invisible Wife had gone to the trouble of getting a sideswept multi-chignon hairdo and a Rue St. Honoré Chloe dress with enormous padded shoulders surmounted by piles of beading sewn on as thick as the topping on a peach melba precisely in order to cease being invisible. But from the moment the social current swept her into the path of Her Husband's business friend Earl, her intracranial alarm system warned her that *it* would happen, nonetheless.

After all, she had only been introduced to Earl four times in the past, at four different parties, and this time Her Husband was in another room.

"Hello, Earl," she said clearly and brightly, looking him straight in the eyes.

Earl's lips spread across his face in a great polyurethaned smile. But his eyes were pure panic. They contracted into two little round balls, like a pair of Gift Shop Lucite knickknacks. "Mayday!" they said. "Code Blue! I've met this woman somewhere, but who inna namea Christ is she?"

"Ohh!" he said. "Ahh! Howya doin'! Yes!—"

The little Lucite balls were bouncing all over her, over her hairdo, chignon by chignon, over her blazing shoulders, her dress, her Charles Jourdan shoes, searching for a clue.

"How're the children!" he exclaimed finally, taking a desperate chance.

This was the deepest wound of all for the Invisible Wife. The man had just passed his eyes over $1,650 worth of Franco-American chic and decided that the main thing about her was . . . she looked *matronly.*

How're the children . . . "They've got Legionnaire's disease," she wanted to say, because she knew these people didn't listen to the Invisible Wife. But she went ahead and did the usual.

"Oh, they're fine," she said.

"That's great!" Earl said. "That's great!" He kept saying "That's great" and looking straight through her, frantically trying to devise some way to remove himself from her presence before somebody he knew approached and he was faced with the impossible task of *introducing* her.

At dinner the Invisible Wife sat next to a man who was an investment counselor with an evident interest in convertible debentures. *Convertible debentures!* An adrenal surge of hope rose in the Invisible Wife. Somewhere down Memory Lane she had actually picked up a conversational nugget concerning convertible debentures. This nugget had to do with an extraordinary mathematician from MIT named Edward O. Thorp who, using computers, had devised an *extrinsic formula* for beating the stock market by playing convertible debentures. So she introduced her conversational nugget—Edward O. Thorp and the Convertible Debentures—into the conversation. She dropped it in, just so, ever so lightly; for, being a veteran of dinners like this, she knew that a woman can ask questions, introduce topics, interject the occasional *bon mot,* even deliver a punch line now and again, but she is not to launch into disquisitions or actually *tell long stories* herself.

"Edward O. Thorp!" the Investment Counselor said. "Oh my God!" —and the Invisible Wife was pleased to see that this topic absolutely delighted the Investment Counselor. He launched into an anecdote that lit up his irises like a pair of bed-lamp high-intensity bulbs. There is nothing that a man hungers for more at dinner than to dominate the conversation in his sector of the table.

The Invisible Wife soon noticed, however, that when the man sitting on the other side of her turned their way to listen in, the Investment Counselor looked right past her and directed the entire story into *the man's* face. Not only that, when this man was distracted for a moment by the woman on his other side, the Investment Counselor stopped talking, as if his switch had been turned off. He stopped in mid-sentence, and his eyes clouded up, and he just waited, with his mouth open.

After all, why waste a terrific yarn on an Invisible Wife?

Boyhood Dreams

"A sniper? The media coverage is good—but when it's over, they throw you in the nuthouse, and that's that. Me, I want to go to Europe and kidnap industrialists for the Revolution and write a book about it and make a lot of money."

The Lower Classes

No. 1. The Down-filled People

They wear down-filled coats in public. Out on the ski slopes they look like hand grenades. They have "audio systems" in their homes and know the names of hit albums. They drive two-door cars with instrument panels like an F–16's. They like High-Tech furniture, track lighting, glass, and brass. They actually go to plays in New York and follow professional sports. The down-filled men wear turtleneck sweaters and Gucci belts and loafers and cover parts of their ears with their hair. The down-filled women still wear cowl-necked sweaters and carry Louis Vuitton handbags. The down-filled people strip wood and have interior walls removed. They put on old clothes before the workmen come over. In the summer they like cabins on fresh water and they go hiking. They regard *Saturday Night Live* and Steve Martin as funny. They say "I hear you," meaning "I understand what you're saying." They say "Really," meaning "That's right." When down-filled strangers are at a loss for words, they talk about real-estate prices.

The Lower Classes

No. 2. Bliss Soho Boho

Oh, to be young and come to New York and move into your first loft and look at the world with eyes that light up even the rotting fire-escape railings, even the buckling pressed-tin squares on the ceiling, even the sheet-metal shower stall with its belly dents and rusting seams, the soot granules embedded like blackheads in the dry rot of the window frames, the basin with the copper-green dripping-spigot stains in the cracks at the bottom, the door with its crowbar-notch history of twenty-five years of break-ins, the canvas-bottom chairs that cut off the circulation in the sural arteries of the leg, the indomitable roach that appears every morning in silhouette on the cord of the hot plate, the doomed yucca straining for light on the windowsill, the two cats nobody ever housebroke, the garbage trucks with the grinder whine, the leather freaks and health-shoe geeks, the punkers with chopped hair and Korean warm-up jackets, the herds of Uptown Boutique bohemians who arrive every weekend by radio-call cab, the bag ladies who sit on the standpipes swabbing the lesions on their ankles—oh, to be young and in New York and to have eyes that light up all things with the sweetest and most golden glow!

The Lower Classes

No. 3. Victims of Inflation

"So I go to the place and I tell the guy I want four of those captain's swivel seats for my van, in leather, to go with the lounge banquette underneath the thermo bay in back, and you know what he tells me? One-half down, 20 percent interest on the balance for two years on a five-year payout basis with a $750 balloon payment at the end!"

"I hear you. This dude who's giving my wife flying lessons, he says he's gonna start charging $35 an hour. I told him he can fly that one right up the freaking pipe!"

The Evolution of the Species

No. 1. Growing Old Gracefully

1879

(". . . as long as they don't think I'm poor . . .")

1979

(". . . as long as they don't think I'm old . . .")

The Evolution of the Species

No. 2. The Eligible Bachelor

1890

("He's rich, he's good-looking, but all he can talk about is patent machinery, unexplosive petroleum, chemical manures, and the Porcellian.")

1980

("He's rich, he's good-looking, but all he can talk about is ludes,
amies, vertical skiing, and skinny boys at Hammamet.")

The Independent Woman

The Independent Woman had not exactly been a ravishing coquette when she was in her teens, and her mother kept urging her to learn a skill. "Something to fall back on," she would say. After all, secretaries, librarians, dental hygienists, double-entry bookkeepers, and reading-disability therapists didn't starve . . .

But the Independent Woman wasn't buying any of that. In college she stuck to courses like Painting and Sculpture in the Age of Reason and Romanticism and the Lake Poets.

Just as her mother had feared, no law or medical student from Harvard or even Penn was swept away by the Independent Woman's charms. After college she had to take a job as an editorial assistant on a magazine, editorial assistant being the title given to girls who couldn't type, take dictation, or keep double-entry books, and who were, in fact, glorified office girls. The men referred to them as cupcakes and lamb chops.

But the Independent Woman wasn't buying any of that. She became one of the leaders of the movement within the office to end sexual stereotyping. Henceforth, female workers would be allowed to wear pants and shirts and other non-girlish gear in order to cease being sex objects. As for herself, the Independent Woman favored roomy corduroys, oversized sweaters, and crepe-soled shoes.

Soon she realized that she looked not so much independent as dowdy, even in the eyes of the other women. So, by and by, now that she was pushing thirty, the Independent Woman decided to cease being a sex object in the same way the other women in the office were ceasing: i.e., by wearing jeans or Cacharel slacks that cleaved the declivities fore and aft and turtleneck jerseys two sizes too small that brought her aureolae out in high relief.

The Independent Woman was married to the assistant comptroller. He kept telling her she had "a terrific body," one of several things she despised him for. Whenever he called her after nightfall from Minneapolis or Kansas City or wherever to say that this or that office manager wanted him to stay over for dinner, meaning that he wouldn't be able to catch a plane back until the morning, and that she, by herself, would have to eat the dinner she had just spent three hours fixing—to the accompaniment of their daughter's whines—he would ask her if she had washed his socks and boxer shorts, had the fuel line on the Torino wagon fixed, or done anything about the bagworms in the cedar bushes. The only person he ever talked to as a social or spiritual equal was the daughter, who had only to force a laugh or two in order to put him in Male Ego Heaven.

The Independent Woman wasn't buying any of that. She had already read a lot of Doris Lessing and Simone de Beauvoir when Millett, Greer, Friedan, and the rest came along, and all of them were marching to her drummer. One day she told her husband she had lived the past ten years completely on his terms, as his laundress, seamstress, station-wagon hacker, gardener, nurse, nanny, and sometime household sex aid. She intended to live the next ten years on her own terms. Whereupon she walked out.

The next few months were exhilarating for the Independent Woman. She joined the EXSTASI organization (Ex-Slaves' Therapy and Socialization Institute), where she was the star of more than one marathon encounter session with her stories of the comptroller and his Rutgers, '52, assumptions about marriage.

Soon enough, however, there was nothing more to tell. Everybody at EXSTASI was much more interested in a new member who was married to a famous semiotic philosopher who insisted that she wear angora-trimmed peekaboo lingerie—which he obtained by mail order under a false name—and put on high heels and jump up and down on a pillow on the floor while he stretched out on the bed in a woman's housecoat he had shoplifted from a local church's Slightly Soiled Shop.

But the Independent Woman wasn't about to buy the likes of that. She said goodbye to EXSTASI and went off on her own and took stock of things. She was now forty, an unemployed editorial assistant, with no husband, living in a one-room apartment built to motel specifications, meaning that the kitchen was a converted closet and the bathroom was a plasterboard box inserted into the living-room space. She began to ponder the old saying "It's no use being more than ten minutes ahead of the times."

The Famous Writer
on the College Lecture Circuit

". . . so we are confronted once again with the duality, the bifurcation, the existential dilemma of the writer's task in America, and . . ."

("The little blonde bud from the creative-writing class is a sure thing, but she'll insist on a lot of literary talk first . . . The big redhead on the lecture committee will spare me that, but she talks to me as if I'm seventy years old . . . Little Bud? . . . or Big Red? . . .)

The Generation Gap

On Parents Day

"Puh-leeze, Mummy, nobody wants to
hear about coke, Acapulco, or Fleetwood Mac."

Success Stories

No. 1. The Modern Churchman

He was a socially acceptable but obscure minister to the Tassel
Loafer & Tennis Lesson Set until the day in 1975 when he announced
that he was a pederast. He not only announced it, he enunciated his
theory that the sexual life of the child was an essential part of, not an
obstacle to, the spiritual life of the child, and that anyone who doubted
that God had created a link of sexual attraction between generations
was an upland Tennessee aborigine. Half of his congregation walked
out, but the other half was stimulated by the television coverage. The
diocesan governors had long been troubled by declining church
membership and felt that here, at last, was a Modern Churchman who
could Reach the Urban Young People. Emboldened by a measure of
fame and official support, he enunciated the theory that terrorists were
God's Holy Beasts, arguing that Jesus had entered the temple with a
flog or cat-o'-nine-tails, according to which Renaissance painting one
looked at, to drive the moneychangers out and that the Mexican artist
David Alfaro Siqueiros had once led a machine-gun raid on the home
of Leon Trotsky. He was a great supporter of the arts, and in his home,
an old carriage house redone in nail patterns by Ronaldo Clutter, the
interior designer, the painting frame had replaced the cross as a
religious symbol. When he held a Holy Roller Disco Night in the
sanctuary and urged the recitation of the prayer book "in tongues," he
was featured in the Religion sections of both *Time* and *Newsweek*, and
his elevation to bishop was said to be imminent.

Success Stories

No. 2. The Anchorman

He graduated from drama school and looked for parts in television. Because he had prognathous jaws like a cowboy's and every cilium of his light-brown hair seemed to be nailed into his skull for keeps, he was steered into the news department. At first, like all beginning newscasters, he had to leave the building. He had to go out and stand in front of City Hall or the hotel where the strike negotiations were taking place or the hospital where the first successful transplant of a lamb's cartilage into a human knee joint was achieved or an apartment building where a three-year-old boy fell five stories and was miraculously caught by an unemployed mason's lumper who was lifting weights in the areaway. He would stand in front of the building and hold a microphone covered in black styrofoam and recite AP or UPI copy about the event. He could do this without skipping a beat, and he maintained his head of hair nearly intact, and soon he did not have to leave the building any more. He was promoted to the anchor desk of the station's six o'clock news broadcast, where he reads the AP and UPI copy from the Teleprompter. Only two things stand in the way of his goal of reaching the network news desk. One is the Anchorwoman, a fireproof blonde who is so aggressive, such a nutcracker, that she terrifies him. His on-air Happy Hour Chitchat with her sounds as if it is being extracted by water torture. The other is the ever-so-imperceptibly widening part in his hair. But he finds that if he shampoos at 3:30 p.m. with Pantene ultra-body and blows it dry with a Continental Pro-style dryer on the hot setting, no one is the wiser.

Primitive Cultures

Professor Nkhrani Emu
Chairman, Department of Anthropology
University of Chembuezi
Babuelu, Chembuezi

Most Esteemed Professor:

As you know, dear Sir, our research team is approaching the end of its field study of "The Sexual Mores of the Americans." I hereby request, most respectfully, that we be granted an extension of the term of our project and a renewal of funding for this work. It is impossible for anyone in a society such as ours to envision from afar the bizarre sexual customs, practices, and rituals to be observed among the American people.

In the republic's largest city, New York, the most prestigious form of entertainment takes place in theaters that have been converted to

dance halls. Hundreds of young males may be seen dancing with one another to flashing lights and recorded music in a homoerotic frenzy, while prominent citizens, including politicians, lawyers, financiers, and upper-class matrons, as well as every sort of well-known figure in the arts, most of them heterosexual, look on, apparently greatly stimulated by the atmosphere. This is described in the native press as "disco fever."

In fact, the mores that have grown up among the Americans concerning homosexuality are apt to be most baffling to the investigator first arriving from a society such as ours. In the United States it is the homosexual male who takes on the appearance that in our society is associated with heterosexual masculinity. Which is to say, he wears his hair short in a style known as the *crew cut* or *butch cut*; he wears the simple leather jacket, sleeveless shirt, crew sweater, or steel-toed boot of the day laborer, truck driver, soldier, or sailor; and, if he exercises, he builds up the musculature of his upper arms and chest. The heterosexual male, by contrast, wears long hair, soft open-throated shirts that resemble a woman's blouse, necklaces, gold wristwatches, shapeless casual jackets of a sort worn also by women; and if he exercises, he goes in for a feminine form of running called *jogging*.

The most popular periodicals in America consist of photographs of young women with gaping pudenda and text of a purportedly serious nature, such as interviews with presidents of the republic (!). These are known as "one-hand magazines."

It is the custom throughout the native schools of America to give *sex education* in the classroom to children by the age of thirteen. The children are taught that sexual intercourse is natural, beautiful, and the highest expression of human love. They are also taught that sexual energy is one of a person's most powerful and creative forces, that it will find expression in some form, that it should not be denied. Yet the Americans are at the same time baffled by the fact that the number of pregnancies out of wedlock among schoolgirls rises continually. In this the Americans are somewhat like the Kombanda tribesmen of our country, who, ignorant of the causal relation of activities separated by time, believe that pregnancy is caused by the sun shining on the bare midsections of females of a certain age. The administrators of the American schools remain bewildered, saying that in the sex-education classes females are given pamphlets clearly outlining birth-control procedures. At the same time, their own records show that only a fraction of American secondary-school graduates can read.

So, most revered Sir, we beseech your support in obtaining for us the resources to complete our work. You will recall, Sir, pointing out to us the importance of Diedrich's discovery of the Luloras, the tribe that made its women climb trees and remain there throughout their menstrual periods. Well, Sir—in all humility!—we are convinced that through our work here we have uncovered a yet more primitive layer in the anthropology of human sexual evolution.

Your worshipful student and friend,
Pottho Mboti

New York City
United States of America

The Secret Heart
of the New York Culturatus

He's anti-Nuke, like everybody else, but he wishes the movement wasn't so full of earnest California types playing guitars and singing those dreadful Pete Seeger Enlightened Backpacker songs—all those women with snap-around denim skirts and low-heeled shoes and honest calves and their poor wimp husbands with their round eyeglasses and droopy beards and their babies strapped to their chests by some sort of papoose rig and spitting up natural-food mush onto their workshirts.

He's for human rights and he's against repression, but somehow he can't get excited about the Boat People: they're a greedy grasping little race that refuses to be assimilated into the new order. Besides, the subject encourages revisionism about the war in Vietnam.

It's tacky to use terms like "Middle America" and "the silent majority." They're so *sixties,* so out of date. He calls them "the fly-over people" instead. They're the people you fly over on the way to Los Angeles.

He doesn't start sentences with "hopefully." He doesn't wear tennis shirts with stripes on them. He doesn't rent summer places north of Route 27. He stopped buying Bolla wines even before they started advertising on television, and he stopped buying bell-bottomed pants two years ago. "Christ," he says to himself, "my radar is fantastic!"

The other day he and his friends were doing the usual, standing up for gay rights, blah-blah-blah, and he could see the maid staring at him. He was so goddamned embarrassed! She was probably wondering if he was *one of them!*

He *loved* the gasoline shortage. All those ethnoproles, who come barreling into Manhattan from Queens in their Coupes de Ville and Monte Carlos with their elephant-collar sport shirts open to the thoracic box, the better to reveal the religious medals twinkling in their chest hair, went back down into the subway where they belonged.

He has an apartment with pure-white walls and a living room with about 4,000 watts worth of R–30 spotlights encased in white cannisters suspended from ceiling tracks and a set of Corbusier bentwoods, which no one ever sits in because they catch you like a karate chop in the small of the back but which remain on the premises because they are in the permanent design collection of the Museum of Modern Art. He has a set of Mies van der Rohe S-shaped tubular-steel cane-bottomed dining-room chairs, which are among the most famous chairs of the twentieth century but also among the most disastrously designed, so that at least one guest always pitches face forward into the lobster bisque. The only decorations are of the Honest Toiler sort, such as the wood-fire-kiln Swedish pots in the living room and the eighteenth-century toolheads, suitably blackened, mounted on the walls of the kitchen. He has a thin wife, starved to near-perfection. He's very proud of the place and likes to invite people over.

The Lord's Work

"... and his lord answered and said unto the servant who had buried his talent, his piece of gold, in the ground: 'Thou *wick*ed and *sloth*ful *ser*vant! Thou *knew*est that I reap where I sowed not and gather where I have not strewed. Thou oughtest therefore to have put my money to the exchangers, and *then* at my coming I should have received my *own* . . . *with interest!'* Now, friends, if you've got your money lying around in a passbook savings account down at the bank . . . *you* . . . are like that *wick*ed *ser*vant! *You* . . . have got your *gold* . . . *stuck* in the *ground!* Wouldn't you rather be able to answer, in the Final Hour, when the Last Questions are asked: 'Oh, *yes*, Lord! I took *my gold* . . . *out* of the passbook savings account! I put *my gold* . . . *into* the Gospel Money Market Fund! Fourteen-point-five percent per annum as of June 15! Interest *com*pounded daily! Withdrawals in part or in full . . . at *any* time! Check-writing privileges . . . *of* course! Bank by wire . . . *a*vailable! Call me tonight, toll free—the Reverend Bob Lee Boyd, Gospel Money Market Fund, *In*corporated—and wake up to*morrow* . . . on the *side* . . . of the *An*gels! This is not an offering, which can be made by formal prospectus only."

4   The Man Who Always
Peaked Too Soon

IN 1964
I CAME OUT AGAINST
THE WAR IN VIETNAM ...
AND I STARTED DOING A NITRO
AND GELIGNITE NUMBER AND I
CALLED FOR THE DESTRUCTION OF
THE UNIVERSITIES IN THEIR PRESENT
FORM ... NOBODY HAILED ME AS A
New left Revolutionary
HOWEVER ... THEY CALLED ME A NUT.
... I GOT THREE YEARS, SUSPENDED.

THREE
YEARS LATER
THE SAME THING
GOT YOU ON
THE COVER OF
Time

BUT
NOT ME,
HOWEVER.

IN 1973... AS YOU CAN SEE...
I GOT INTO WING=COLLAR SHIRTS
AND DOUBLE=BREASTED WAISTCOATS
AND SENIOR SERVICE CIGARETTES
AND MARTINIS AND SHORT HAIR
SLICKED BACK LIKE THE
Patent Leather Kids
... I BOUGHT TWO SLAVES
IN THE HILLS OF MOROCCO
AND SOME MALLET=STEVENS
EASY CHAIRS IN PARIS...

MORAL:
DON'T DO WHAT
YOU SEE ME DOING...
Wait
THREE YEARS

UNTIL... OH...
ABOUT 1976.

5 Portraits

Lillian Carter

Edward Kennedy

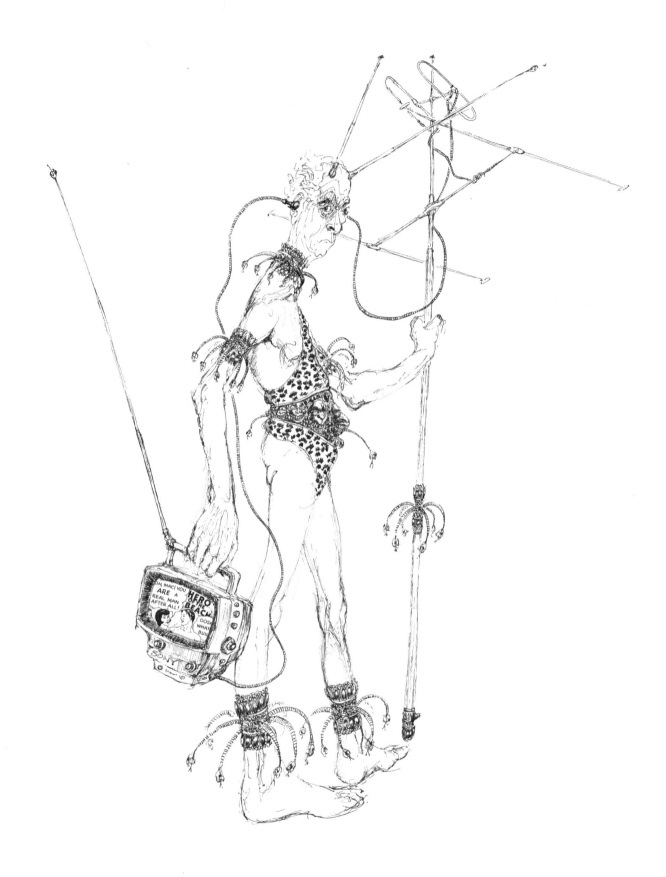

Marshall McLuhan

Hugh Hefner

Carol Doda

Duncan Sandys

Andy Warhol

6 The World of Art

Artists from Cincinnati and Cleveland, hot off the Carey airport
bus, line up in Soho looking for the obligatory loft.

I'm Still a Virgin. (Where's the Champagne?)

Proper attire for the artist who refuses to sell out but wants to go to the black-tie Patrons Night opening at the Museum of Modern Art all the same.

Puzzle Picture

In the late 1960s the Conceptualists began to ask: Suppose the greatest artist in the history of the world, impoverished and unknown, had been sitting at a table in the old Automat at Union Square, helping himself to some free water and hoping to cop a leftover crust of toasted corn muffin or a few abandoned translucent chartreuse waxed beans or some other item of that amazing range of Yellow Food the Automat went in for—and suddenly he got the inspiration for the greatest work of art in the history of the world? Possessing not even so much as a pencil or a burnt match, he dipped his forefinger into the glass of water and began recording this greatest of all inspirations, this high point in the history of man as a sentient being, on a paper napkin, with New York tap water as his paint. In a matter of seconds, of course, the water had diffused through the paper and the grand design vanished, whereupon the greatest artist in the history of the world slumped to the table and died of a broken heart, and the manager came over, and he thought that here was nothing more than a dead wino with a wet napkin. Now, the question was: Would that have been the greatest work of art in the history of the world or not?

Great Ideas of Western Man

Hitch your wagon to a star.
—*Ralph Waldo Emerson*

The corporations discover Culture, and the Transcendental Can Corporation begins its Great Ideas series, featuring a quotation from Emerson underneath a cubist horse strangling on a banana.

When Flat Was God

The position the artists took after Clement Greenberg set forth his theory of Flatness.

7 The Bohemian Hedge

The Bohemian Hedge . . .

against the resentments of an egalitarian world.

As she told the interviewer for the Lifestyle section (*nee* the Women's section), she may be a debutante, but she's not the kind you think. She's tired of so-called coming-out balls, where you dance the Mexican hat dance to the music of a so-called society band while your parents stand around the edges talking to a lot of old ladies in orange-juice-colored dresses. She's tired of cotillions and hunt cups and smart weekends. You want to know what she did last weekend? She spent last weekend down at the daycare center . . . looking after the most beautiful black children . . . and learning from them, of course . . . She turned up for interview with the Lifestyle reporter in bellbottomed blue jeans and a cotton blouse open to just below the sternum. She left her hair long, natural, primitive, uncoifed. All she did was lay it out on an ironing board and give it the once-over with an iron on the silks-and-rayon setting to bring up the sheen a bit.

The Bohemian Hedge . . .

against being thought old-fashioned.

He doesn't preach *at* the young people in his church, he preaches *through* them. He is their voice, and they are his. Tonight he's playing the banjo at a hootenanny in the activities center. Tomorrow afternoon he'll be at the lake on his water skis speaking to the young people over a bullhorn.

The Bohemian Hedge...

against age.

He's got pyramid panels in his bells and a spray-can fit in the seat.
(How old could he *be*?)

The Bohemian Hedge . . .

against baby, daddy, the mortgage, the Aspen, the
hideous Singing Fountain at the main hall intersection in
the shopping mall, and the dentist who sends comic cards
to remind you of the family's six-month checkups.

She's not suburban; she's bohemian.

8 California

The Pump House, Windansea Beach, La Jolla, 1965.

Wah Ching boy, Chinatown, San Francisco, 1969. Hong Kong-born Chinese gang members were the last teenagers in America to wear the teased pompadour with the ducktail.

Harvey's Drive-in, Firestone Boulevard, Downey, California.

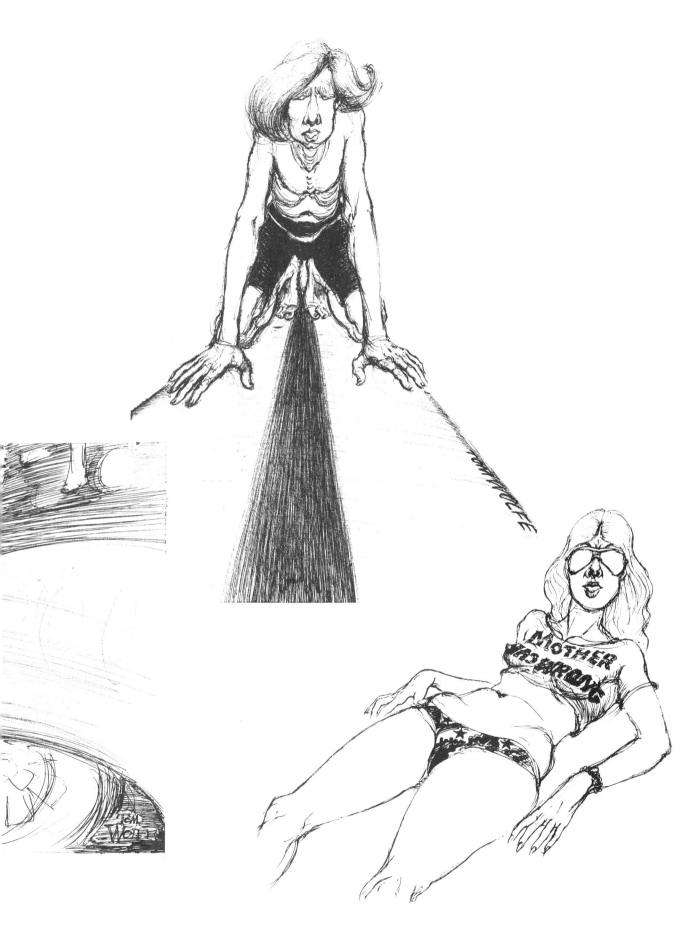

93

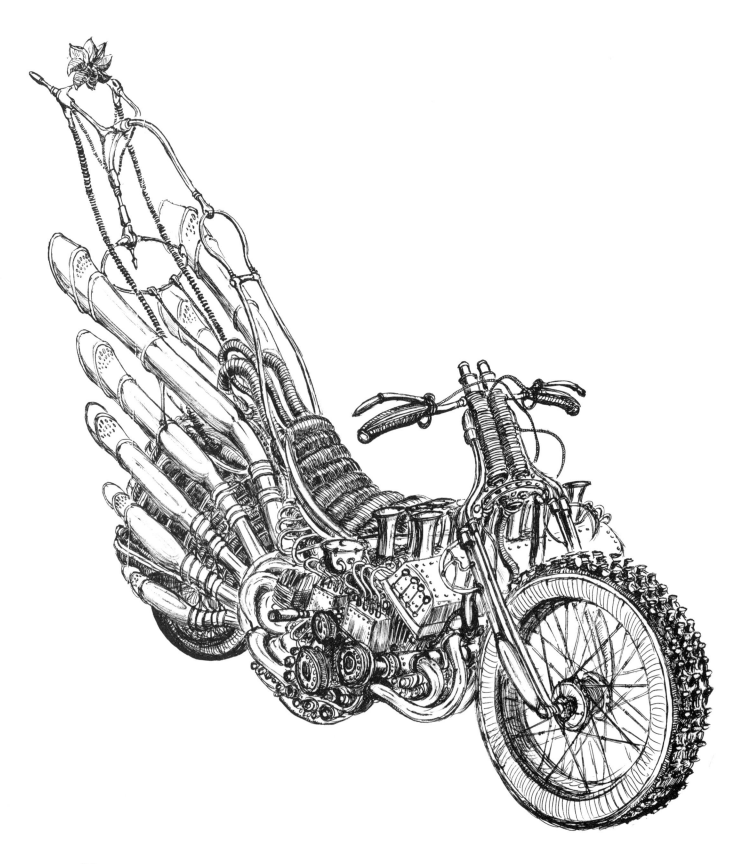

9   England

A Private Game

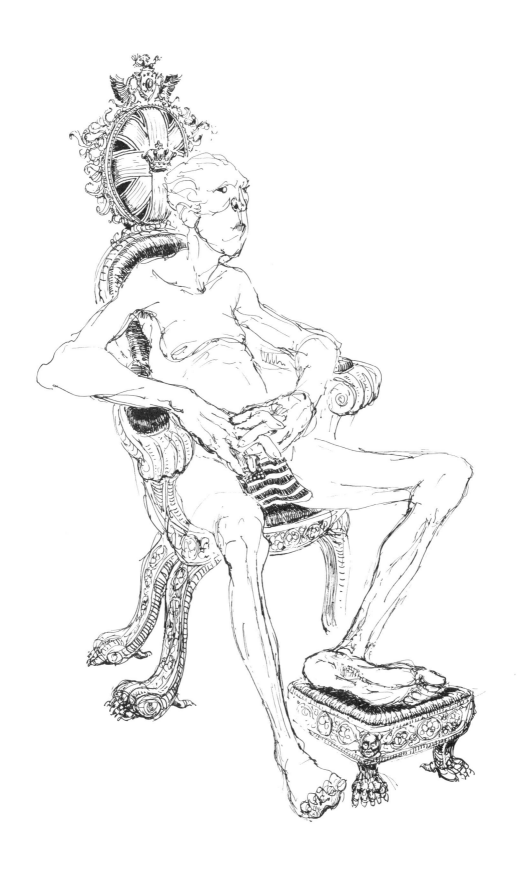

The Mid-Atlantic Man

The Skinhead

10 New York

The Seven Graces of New York

The Cabdriver

The Dock Porter

The Parking Lot Attendant

The Maître d'

The Hat-Check Girl

The Tour Guide

The Traffic Patrolman

The Village Book Shop

In Back

Up Front

The Realist

Thomas Wolfe

Save!
COSMETIC
TOILET
HEALTH
SUNDRIE

Tom Wolfe
PROP.

Utility
workers
Third Avenue
February 1974

Tom Wolfe

The Convention

114

The Monkey Dinner

The Melting Pot

The Photograph Hound (successor to the autograph hound)

Aqueduct Race Track

Out shopping.

Scholars on the subway express to the track.

The Sportsmen, who come to the track and watch the races on closed-circuit television near the betting windows.

The Sport of Kings: riding the losing jockeys after the race.

The Stooper, scavenging the litter for inadvertently discarded winning tickets.